Bloodlines

Other Books by Andy Brown

Full Poetry Collections
Exurbia (Worple Press, 2014)
The Fool and the Physician (Salt, 2012)
Goose Music (Salt, 2008, with John Burnside)
Fall of the Rebel Angels: Poems 1996-2006 (Salt, 2006)
Hunting the Kinnayas (Stride, 2004)
From a Cliff (Arc, 2002)
The Wanderer's Prayer (Arc, 1999)
West of Yesterday (Stride, 1998)

Poetry Chapbooks and Pamphlets
Watersong (Shearsman, 2015)
Woody Alliance Laundered (Argotist Ebooks, 2011)
The Storm Berm (tall-lighthouse, 2008)
The Trust Territory (Heaventree, 2005)
of Science (Worple Press, 2001, with David Morley)
The Sleep Switch (Odyssey, 1996)

Editor
A Body of Work: Poetry and Medical Writing (Bloomsbury, 2016, with Corinna Wagner)
The Writing Occurs As Song: a Kelvin Corcoran Reader (Shearsman, 2014)
The Allotment: new lyric poets (Stride, 2006)
Binary Myths 1 & 2: correspondences with poets and poet-editors (Stride, 2004)

BLOODLINES

POEMS

ANDY BROWN

First published in 2018 by
Worple Press
Achill Sound, 2b Dry Hill Road
Tonbridge
Kent TN9 1LX.
www.worplepress.co.uk

Cover image: adimas – stock.adobe.com

Printed by imprintdigital
Upton Pyne, Exeter
www.imprintdigital.com

Typeset and cover design by narrator typesetters and designers
www.narrator.me.uk
info@narrator.me.uk
033 022 300 39

ISBN: 978-1-905208-40-1

Acknowledgements

Special thanks are due to the editors of the following publications where some of these poems—or earlier versions of them—appeared:

'The Splinter' in *The Broadsheet*; 'Anatomy for the Blind' in *Cordite Poetry Review* (Aus); 'Surgery Operation' in the *International Times*; 'A Doctour of Phisik' in *The London Magazine*; 'Genetics' in *Magma*; 'Keystones' in *Other Voices International*; '*Ecorché*' in *Poor Yorick* and *A Body of Work* (Bloomsbury); 'A Story about Teeth' in *Qualia and Other Wildlife*; 'A Sick Lady and her Doctor, 1657', 'Acute Myocardial Infarction', 'Berserk' and 'Surgery Operation' in *Stride Magazine*; 'Shield Bugs' and 'The Crowd' in *Under the Radar*; 'Public Speaking' in *The Warwick Review* and *A Body of Work*; and 'Self-Portrait at Fifty' in the *York Literary Review*.

'Committal' was commissioned by Michael McKimm for *The Tree Line*, an anthology to celebrate the New Peoples' Charter for Woodlands (Worple, 2017).

The sequence 'Bloodlines', about the Cornish-born physician and pioneer of blood circulation, Richard Lower, was commissioned for the anthology *Into the Roots* (Penryn Press, 2015). 'The Broad Street Pump', 'The Unnamable Taxonomy', 'The Coroner's Ballad', 'The Ballad of the Sexton', 'Bury Fields' and 'The Flying Toilets of Kibera' were originally published in the chapbook, *Watersong* (Shearsman, 2015); thanks here to Tony Frazer and Kelvin Corcoran.

With great gratitude to Beatriz Villacañas Palomo for permission to include my version of '*Incineracion*' ('Cremation') by Juan Antonio Villacañas, and to Victor Rodriguez Nuñez for permission to include versions of his poems '*Hospitales*' ('Hospitals') and '*Arte Poetica*?' ('A Leap Year Nose').

With thanks to Exeter University for seed-funding a research project on poetry, water and sanitation. Enormous thanks to Christopher Southgate, who played both midwife and godfather to many of these poems and knew when and how to resuscitate those that were ailing. Thanks to Marc Woodward for his astute comments and on-going collaborations, and to Peter Carpenter for his generosity and acute editorial eye. Lastly to Corinna Wagner who made the many research trips to medical museums and archives the joy that they were.

About the Author

Andy Brown is Professor of English & Creative Writing at Exeter University. His recent poetry books include *Exurbia* (Worple Press, 2014); *The Fool and the Physician* (Salt, 2012); *Goose Music* (with John Burnside, Salt, 2008) and *Fall of the Rebel Angels: Poems 1996–2006* (Salt, 2006). He recently co-edited *A Body of Work: Poetry and Medical Writing* (with Corinna Wagner, Bloomsbury, 2016) and edited and contributed to *The Writing Occurs As Song: a Kelvin Corcoran Reader* (Shearsman, 2015). He is a performing singer-songwriter, manages the independent *Maquette Press* and divides his time between Devon and Brittany.

Contents

I. Public Speaking

Genetics

Like chromosomes beneath a microscope
white contrails wind across a turquoise sky.

On the concrete of their grey suburban yard
the family lounges, sipping sodas, licking ices.

Above, their patch of heaven throbs. Summer
has descended like a tedious uncle, boring them

with the wilting force of never-ending stories:
adventures, misadventures, how he burned

in the stock market crash. Blistered berries
shrivel on the bush. The kids breed stripes

behind the picket fence, fighting over the hose.
Mum fans her face with glossy magazines;

dad struggles with the morning's crossword:
'8 letters. *Oppressive Climate*:
                    H blank A blank Dubya blank blank E…?'

Berserk

Ber serkr: bear-shirted, dressed in bear pelts

i.m. Iain Potts

You said the word *berserk* came from the Norse—
a name for Viking warriors who fought
with unrestrained hostility. *Berserkers.*

To 'go berserk' was *hamask*, shifting shape,
becoming bear, blind drunk on reindeer piss
imbued with psychotropic residues
of fly agaric—toxic *Amanita*—

as if those myths gave you the go-ahead
to drink and smoke, do all the dope you could,
then do more drugs to help you down again
before the doctors gave you pills and said

'Give up before you die…' and you gave up
just long enough for us to watch you lope
off to the woods to shape-shift one last time.

The Splinter

I don't remember when or how it found
its way beneath the surface of my skin—
loafing on a wooden bench, or sliding
down the rotten rails above the steps
at the station after school was over,

but there it was, this spike of pine, this spine
of wood, lodged in the softest, hidden flesh,
the *oubliette* between my teenage buttocks—
invisible, subcutaneous, immense:
a Highlander's caber, a redwood's trunk.

'What's happened now; what have you done?'
my mother asked, knowingly, as she
rose from her knees and the loaded wash
to watch me limp pathetically inside.
I tried in vain to cover up my tears

and though I understand now how she wanted
to balance my moans with laughter when I said
I was mortally wounded, spiked, defiled,
she led me to the bath and ordered 'Soak!
I'll be back with a needle once it's swelled.'

O punctured self... how could I ever crawl
back from that? Naked, down on all fours,
arse in the air and her beatific,
poker face behind the gleaming tweezers:
'Oh honestly, *that* tiny little thing?'

Shield Bugs

for Sue Chedzoy

I like to think these raspberry canes are *mine*,
cut in winter, weeded through the spring,
trained across the hopeful wires of summer
to yield up punnets of come-again fruit—

but this September morning they're alive
with shield bugs. As I hunt beneath the leaves
for the hanging gems of raspberries, the ground
reveals itself as home to a crawling swarm.

These jade Egyptian scarabs of 'my patch'
have shown themselves to be the rightful heirs
of these allotted yards of garden plot
and will remain so after we have gone:

myself and 'Sue the Sheds', our neighbour Ralf
who taught me not to plant my beans before
the frosts of May, and Jim whose heart packed up
last March and no one ever sees here anymore.

Keystones

i.m. Emily Riall

The day you decided the darkness would win
and yoked yourself to a vanishing point
beyond the reach of our reckoning
you answered the one binding question.

But now, as you begin to settle down
into what we keep in mind of you, and we
reconcile ourselves to asking questions
we never wished to ask, a scar of absence

arouses there inside us *Hows & Whys*:
how the future grew too big, too fast for you;
how you fought it with your smile alone;

why our mistakes are the keystones
in the triumphal arches of our lives
above this road we call Recovery.

Committal

'We all need a second life, the one we have
goes spinning away too soon.'
— John Burnside, 'Nocturne: Christmas, 2012'

Today a teenage girl secured her right
to have herself cryonically preserved

so maybe in five hundred years, or more,
once mutation's mystery has been solved,

her body may be warmed to stir again
and she can live the life she's barely led.

I also wish to carry on, here's how:
inter me deep in loamy woodland soil

then plant a sapling oak above my head,
so hair and skin and bone may be reborn

in twig and leaf, in xylem, riddled bark;
so the seep of muscle and marrow may

replenish soil, feed worm and ant and moth…
and moth feed shrew and shrew feed owl and fox.

No need for messages carved into stone:
Your journey to the spirit world starts here—

just let the faintest hints of musk remain:
that trace and pulse of what we must become.

Twins

for Ali Barnett

The twist began when we were tightly curled
and sharing space behind our mother's navel.

You jumped head first but I, late starter,
followed you out with this kink in my spine

that antispasmodics and paediatric traction
could only part-way straighten.

Twenty years later you jumped so far
you landed on your feet in Western Aus.,

kicking back for months, though soon enough
battling for space in your new suburban home

with four kids, two dogs and a husband out flat
on his back after downing the wages again…

And though the waters of the womb have turned
to oceans between the two of us,

from time to time I feel a push or pull
as if from nowhere—bending down

to tug a weed, or tie a shoe, or simply turning
from the sink when the telephone rings—

and the memory inherent in the spine
kicks out the kink that leaves me on *my* back

as I remind myself it isn't only me
who's had to learn to strengthen the core,

to pull the stomach muscles tight,
to brace the spine and try to stand up tall.

Public Speaking

i.m. Dereke Leslie Brown

i. Public Speaking

My father was a man of very few words
and, curiously, a well-versed public speaker.
He began every speech with the same old joke:
Unaccustomed as I am to public speaking…

before launching into his theme, after dinner
to the Board, a lunch at the Club,
at weddings, birthdays, parties, funerals,
he'd take the stand and roll the old line out.

My father was an orator, self-taught.
His dog-eared copy of *Teach Yourself…*
sits in his scant library—he never was
a letters man and was often quiet at home

or, when on the phone, found chatting hard.
But publicly he wasn't shy. I think of him
the days before a speech, mugging up
on helpful tips from *Teach Yourself:*

*Practice and rehearse your speech at home
or where you'll surely be at ease, in front
of a mirror, your family, or friends…*
this duly noted, circumscribed in pencil.

Appear relaxed, even when you're not…
he's jotted in the margins of
a well-thumbed page on *Building Your Rapport*,
which also recommends to tell a joke:

Unaccustomed as I am to public speaking…

After the brain disease began to make
greater strangers of his mind and tongue,
we picked up only garbled fogs of sound.
Squeeze my hand, we used to say, *if you can hear us, dad,*

then wait in silence for the pressure.
We watched him disappear until he reached
the farthest point and, though I can't recall
his final words, his margin notes will serve:

Address your speech to the person farthest away
to ensure your voice is loud enough to be heard.

ii. Paring

He used to say that every morning shave
was a pleasure a man ought to savour—

a dash around the jowls with the bone-
handled brush, lathering the thickened foam

that turned him into Santa Claus, or Hemingway,
before he whisked the soapy mask away

with a cut-throat and splashed on cologne.
I'd stand there head to waist, looking on

at his newly pink smile, wondering when
this early morning ritual would be mine.

Years on, I hand the razor over, watch how
the nurse erases his five o'clock shadow

and leave the hospice promising myself
to give the beard another month of growth.

iii. The Vacuum

It began with these lapses of mind
he called 'being off with the fairies'—
forgetfulness, staring into space,

strange periods of nothingness at all
while gardening, or playing rounds of golf
in which he had no memory of how
he'd cleared the rough or reached the 18th green.

That was while his mind and tongue still worked
as one, before the vacuum veiled his words
behind the product names on blister packs:

Riluzole for improved nerve transmission,
Citalopram to lift the melancholy,
Fybogel to bulk the liquid food
when he couldn't grip a fork or hold a spoon.

iv. The Shunt

Whether he could hear I couldn't know,
nor whether he remembered these things too,
but I spoke about them to him nonetheless:

the *Airfix* models we had made together
Sunday evenings, sealing our rapport
with pots of paint and dribbling tubes of glue;

the time he found me, midnight, crawling drunk
on the bathroom floor after walking me home
from a party, my toes fixed to the lines
between the slabs;
                       the bicycles we had built
together; the go kart wheels we'd removed
from an old pram and welded to a frame;
fishing trips… and gardening…
how grandad's flowers became his own
and now those flowers were mine;

the birch tree in his garden he'd cut down
when he feared that it might tumble onto the house…
and the new birch tree in my own back yard,
that scuzzy flat I lived in post divorce…

Whether these things mattered didn't matter.
I simply let them slip out
to the sounds of his wheezing,
      the monitor's steady beeps,
            the measured trundle of the pumping shunt.

v. Nightlights

The lanterns in the yard began to glow
recharged on sun stored-up through daylight hours,

flickering like flotillas of spacecraft
that hovered over dad's herbaceous borders.

You were flying back from Australia,
navigating in between the stars

to make it home in time before he died.
I searched the constellations for your plane.

Upstairs in the bedroom his own lights
were petering out. From where I stood

outside, the window had become a screen
on which his film was spooling off.

By midnight you'd arrived, said your goodbyes
but I, too scared to watch, had taken leave.

Along the motorway the lines of cat's eye's
passed exacting judgment on *my* flight.

Excision

He lay his plastered forearm on the bench,
the scribbles of his class just legible—
You skiving bastard!… Loser! … Lots of Luv…

The shift nurse put the rotary saw in gear.
'No need to worry, just relax,' she said,
'the cutter goes no deeper than the cast.'

He tried to disregard the whirring metal,
as it carved a line of dust down to the wrist,
a millimeter proud of helpless skin.

When he came round, to smelling salts, sweet tea,
the cast was bagged, a tattered souvenir—his arm
hirsute, but white, where the summer had missed.

On Septicaemia

When the needle-thin thorn went in under his skin,
he sucked the mingled blood and juice that bloomed
upon his punctured knuckle, removed the barb
and went on plucking—six bitter-sweet bushes
of ripened berries and almost sixty pounds
of bulbous fruit piled up in trugs and buckets.

That evening at the wedding dance he couldn't spin
his girl to salsa, nor shake the bridegroom's hand,
though buckets of claret were dulling the pain
that throbbed through his fingers as in a cartoon.

Awake in bed at 3a.m., weeping like a mother
at a wedding, the tendons and muscle mass
swollen to a baseball catcher's glove, he knew
he'd have to walk to casualty, each footstep
thudding through his hand like kettle drums.

                          On the ward,
his arm raised high inside a padded sling,
the duty nurse slipped a needle in a vein…
'For sugars, cell count, thickness of the plasma.'
Queasily he watched the blood exude
before she introduced the cannula,
the saline and the eager vancomycin,
calm analgesics for his shooting pains.

O gentle nurse… voracious penicillin…
        Sweet anodynes and staining gooseberry juice…
            O undercover passages of blood.

Skin Tag

Blindly it sat
at the nape of her neck—
a miniscule anemone;

a pea-sized nodule
of tissue—the polyp
that our childish fingers

rubbed-up against
as we clung round her neck
like monkeys. *That's where*

they sealed me up,
once they'd finished making me.
Every woman has one…

Our childish eyes widening
in blind trust and wonder.
O soft fibroma,

where are you now?
In what rockpool of dreams
is your pink eye blinking?

Some Sayings About the Hand

after George Szirtes

The hand is river, valley, mountain, moor.
The hand is the claw in its dotage.
It juts from sleeve and cuff in openness, or clenched.
The baton of the hand describes its harmonies.
It pulls back water, like curtains at the grand finalé.
An open hand lets glitches drop.
The hand applauds its other generously.
Its shadow is an empty glove.
We hear its tendons and muscles in the strings' vibrations.
A bird sits in the hand while the bushes rustle.
It is pentagram and ragged flag of dreams.
Its touch lingers, like a painted outline on a Stone Age wall.
The hand rests here, drumming, impatiently
    waiting for your face.

Self Portrait at Fifty

after Rabelais

...and his nipples were Castor and Pollux
and his windpipe was *Blood on the Tracks*,
his bladder and spleen were Hieronymus Bosch.
His eardrum was a sheaf of lyric poems.

And his ribcage was a fossil Stegosaurus
and his calves were the rails of a ladder.
His lips were *Monopoly* hotels
and his blood was hot sauce.

His teeth were a set of white chessmen,
his temples were statues of the Buddha,
his diaphragm was a garden trampoline,
his arms were kestrels hovering in the wind.

And his liver was a case of *grand cru* Medoc.
And his shoulder blades were shoals of mackerel.
His armpits were a dinghy's rusting rowlocks
and his palms were renewable energy.

His gullet was a green-glazed feudal jug
and his eyebrows were padlocks on portholes.
His eyes were sprinkler head *and* shower curtain
and his uvula swung like a punchbag.

His pelvis was a turtle crossing oceans
and his tongue was a fire on the beach.
His lungs were murmurating starlings
and his cheeks were bluffs along a lonely cliff.

His jawbone was a fox's in the grass.
His brain was the Northern Lights.
The nape of his neck was the prow of a boat
and his optic nerves were seaside view-finders.

If he scratched, then his fingers were chopsticks.
If he grumbled, his nose was a walnut.
His pineal glowed like an inglenook.
When he sang, his chest was the Taj Mahal.

His Adam's apple, neck and chin were the Holy Trinity.
The bridge of his nose was a raised hockey stick.
The soles of his feet were dolphins at the wake.
His feet themselves were distant siblings.

His loins were a tooled set of Dickens.
His spermatozoa were teaspoons in a sink.
His bladder was a crystal flute and tumbler
and when he bathed his navel was Hay Tor.

His thighs were Olivier's *Hamlet*
and his nerves were the big wheel and dodgems.
His heels and his toes were a volume of verbs.
His perineum was a bass guitar.

His arteries were earthworms in dark humus.
His tendons and muscles were apples and pears.
His guts were a tarn in the mountains.
and his spinal column was a wishing well...

And every time he tossed a penny in that well,
he always wished for this and this alone:
long life, good health and a heart to fly
the stubborn birdcage of his breastbone.

A Story About Teeth

The schoolboy gladly found himself off school. Yet soon he heard his mother's voice explain exactly what would happen to his teeth. His teeth were far too many, cramped inside the cavern of his mouth and, if he wanted a winning smile, then some of them needed to go; to be pulled; to make space so the rest could grow in line.

They stood in line at the surgery, the schoolboy sucking his thumb, his mother thumbing glossy magazines and, when the dentist's prep nurse came, she called the schoolboy's name and pulled him fast across the polished floor. He felt like he was flying in a dream.

Inside the sterile room, the dentist spoke behind his mask and scrubs. "Bite down on the little rubber block; there's medicine inside a hidden phial. Slip off to sleep and dream of something nice..."

No sooner said, the little black block crunched...

and the whole crowd was cheering wildly as the schoolboy flew towards the goal, the ball at his feet as big as the sun—the glory that awaited him even brighter. But as the hulking goalie flew his line, the schoolboy couldn't see a ball to kick and, taking the goalie's fingers in his mouth, tore into his thumb with teeth the size of sabres...

Inside the car, his mother's face was ripe with shame. Inside the surgery, the dentist's prep nurse pinned the sodden bandage. Inside the schoolboy's mouth, the first taste of a stranger's mingled blood.

II. Bloodlines

Homo naledi

a new species of hominid linking Australopithecus afarensis *and* Homo sapiens. *The bones unearthed in South Africa in 2013 are believed to have been buried ritually some 2 million years ago—the earliest known case of such activity.*

'How much longer will I be able to inhabit the divine sepulchre...'
– John Ashbery

In Gauteng's caves the dons are asking how
the branches of our past converge; if much
connects these buried bones with the longer
lines that lead out from the trees. They will
in time shed light.   It's many years since I
studied bones for my degree, though it may be
some trace of that tuition leaves me able
to picture this new archaeology; to
realize how a creature might inhabit
the ineffable passages of the
past—the gap between what's 'matter', what 'divine';
the meanings of their primal sepulchre.

Human Anatomy Classes

i. Écorché

plaster cast crucifixion of the body of James Legg,
Chelsea Pensioner, hanged for murder Nov 2, 1801,
by Thomas Banks (1735-1805), Royal Academy.

They made me to settle an artists' debate—
my seventy-three-year-old body deposed
from the hangman's gibbet and nailed to a cross
to put the Academics' minds at rest:

the sculptor Banks, the painters Cosway, West.
Gentlemen! Let me help you put it straight:
most paintings of the Crucifixion mask
gross inaccuracies… *physically*, of course.

Captain William Lamb was my undoing;
Lamb who wouldn't meet me in a duel;
Lamb, that 'tyrannical tempered man'
who shunned my guns. I shot *him* in the chest.

I confess: I was melancholy. I was dejected.
I woke like a person surprised from sleep
when matron arrived with my tincture.
The surgeon Joseph Carpue cut *me* down

to put the artists' theory to the test.
He took my body from the hanging place,
then winched me up until my muscles slumped
into the proper pose of crucifixion.

There I hung until my carcass cooled
and when I'd cooled, he flayed me so that Banks
could make his cast. (West said he'd never *seen*
the human hand till then.) And here I hang, still,

in the way of our Saviour—this mock
James Legg—survivor of the noose, the knife,
the cross—where curious Anatomy meets Art,
where Religion meets Justice, and firm proof.

ii. The Crowd

In paintings of those ancient operations—
an amputated leg, a tooth excised,
the rapid removal of tumour tissue
from the numbed and pendent breast—

there's always a dark congregation,
their faces lit around the patient's bench:
nurses with salvers of instruments;
a butcher with a hammer and a saw;

the quack and his gaggle of charlatans
smiling down the guy-with-toothache's gullet;
periwigged practitioners; students of the noble art
decked out in capes & ruffs,

each leaning in on individual pain
to learn the workings of the mimic muscles
in the cheek; to see the maestro score and saw
before he lets the scabbed limb drop

into the waiting bucket in the dust.
And at the heart of this collective gawp,
the brandied man, the woman coshed
with mandrake, privately lit from within.

iii. Anatomy for the Blind

Black and white photograph of a 'talk-and-touch'
session for the blind, about human anatomy, held
in an art gallery, 1913.

Beneath the languid nudes of Ingres and Renoir,
the Odalisques and Venus on her couch,
the skeleton is already reclined
against the lectern as the doctor starts:

'Gentlemen, explore tonight your sense of touch.
Let the warmth of your fingers and palms
caress the cool crest of this ivory planet.

From the summit of this fragile sphere glide
across the bumps and ridges; understand
the subtle fissures and the secret cracks,

the domed expanse that disappears beneath
itself. Now press your ear against this blade,
which creaks like a ship on shifting waves:

that's the sailboat of the scapula
hitched onto the clavicle's safe cleat.
And here beneath as broad as any barrel,

the ribs—your maker's hoops and staves.
This chilly shaft's the femur, Sir, just like
the cane you'll use to guide yourself away...'

And when the talk is done the blind depart
and just the silent skeleton remains,
sole tenant of this vacant gallery
with paintings neither she nor they can see.

iv. Birthing Machine

Giovanni Antonio Galli (1708–1782)
Glass womb, wooden pelvis, cloth foetus.
Palazzo Poggi, Bologna.

The obstetrician with his team of midwives
stands watchful in his frock coat, wig, cravat,
his hand outstretched towards the fragile dome
of his birth machine, his reproduction womb.

The textile foetus hangs above the pelvis
while blindfold midwives reach inside to feel
the different ways the foetus may be lying:
posterior, transverse, oblique or *breech*.

One day a pregnant woman will lie back—
real flesh and blood and screaming nerves—
as the midwives make the movements they have learned,

feeling for the baby's pressing crown,
while in the obstetrician's leather case
the cold and antiseptic tongs lie waiting.

v. A Sick Lady and Her Doctor, 1657

Painting from the workshop of Franz Van Mieris the Elder,
in which the artist mocks a patient who is not ill, but lovesick.

Survival rates in Europe
have doubled over forty years

because of better treatment,
testing and early diagnosis.

There are literally hundreds of types.
What should you *look for*?

An unexplained aching or pain;
an unusual swelling in the chest;

puckered skin around the mouth,
with blood; a soreness that won't heal

even after several weeks or months
of treatment. It's so important

that you called—swift analysis
and screening can save lives.

vi. *Human Anatomy Classes*

after the anatomical collections at La Specola, Florence
and the Palazzo di Poggi, Bologna

There's years between the class I used to teach—
'Anatomy for Beauty Therapists' at the Tech—
where twenty blank sixteen-year-olds learned the score
of muscles in the leg: *Tibialis, Gastrocnemius, Extensor...*

and these écorché models in the darkened galleries
of *La Specola* and *La Palazzo di Poggi,*
where Ercole Lelli, *direttore di figura,* pulls a rope
to unveil his human waxworks for the Pope...

but everything those girls were made to learn,
to graduate with honours in massage
and muscle tone, smoothing the décolletage,

nutritional advice, conditions of the skin,
begins here with the artfulness of these
uncanny, disclosed bodies, lying at their ease.

Bloodlines

Richard Lower (1631–91), born St. Tudy, Cornwall. Physician. Fellow of the Royal Society. Performed the first blood transfusion experiments in England.

i. Two Mongrels

February. Sixteen fifty-five.
Two mongrels fastened to a surgeon's table,

the blood of the one flowing in to the other
from artery to vein, through cannula and quill.

The donor, having yielded up his kinship,
whimpers, stumbles, dies. The other mongrel

shakes himself and barks, palpably alive.
The surgeon fills his notebook with schemata,

with surgical precisions, the tools required:
'You must bleed a great dog into a smaller,

a mastiff into a cur… Bright red arterial blood
replenishes the dark and venous matter.

Is the life force not to be discovered
in the body? Does it not subsist in blood?'

ii. Bedlam

Watching the flow of the Thames from his lab,
disposing of the dog's corpse in its depths,

the surgeon waits for all the moral protests
to wane, before his efforts turn to human beings.

He bides his time to level with the French
who already 'have hazarded the life of Man'.

He knows transfusion cools a sanguine person;
knows too that this relieves 'extravagant minds'.

He goes to Bedlam, looking for a subject,
if the Governor will allow. He will not:

'Does man not have a soul? What of the lamb?
And what shall arise when the blood of the man

and the blood of the lamb intermingle?
Which part is the animal? Which the man?'

iii. Arthur Coga

Late November. Sixteen sixty-seven.
A crowd of viewers bursting at the doorway.

Arthur Coga, a competent speaker
of Latin, whose brain is 'a little too warm',

sitting with his forearm bared and waiting
and, opposite, a trussed, unknowing lamb.

The surgeon opens the lamb's circulation,
inserts a silver tube into the wound.

Bright liquid falls in silver porringers.
He caps the cannula, addresses Coga,

who dips a knife into the creature's blood,
parts his lips and finds it 'of good relish'.

The lancet snicks a vein on Coga's arm.
Out flow six ounces, mirroring the lamb's.

iv. Which Part is Man?

The surgeon slips a tube in Coga's vein
and caps it... 'linking, my learned gentlemen,

the lamb's blood with the patient's.' He releases
the stoppered conduits; watches the flow.

Coga drinks a glass of wormwood wine,
amuses the audience with Latin quips:

'*Christus est agnus Dei.*' Another glass of wine,
a pipe to smoke. He wanders home.

His appetite is good, his mood undimmed.
He passes a regular stool. But, by night,

the patient is unsettled. 'You've transform'd
me into another species: *Agnus Coga!*

Does the soul not subsist in the body?
Which part of me is animal... Which part is man?'

A Doctour of Phisik

after The Prologue, Canterbury Tales

We took a doctor with us on our way
who understood the laws of surgery

much more than most. There wasn't anyone
with more than him to say on medicine.

He knew about the heavens and had learnt
the precise timings and exact treatments

proscribed by the planets and stars.
He'd read you your medical chart

or horoscope, to find the *What & Why*
of any illness—hot or cold, wet or dry—

where it was seated and what was its form:
blood or bile, melancholy or phlegm.

He was a master! He'd get to the core
of what was up and proffer you the cure

toute suite—his peddlers of potions and balms
were close at hand to grease each other's palms.

He'd studied masters like Dioscorides
and quoted freely from Hippocrates,

Haly, Averroes and Constantine.
I think he was a vegetarian—

he ate small meals and only organic.
He wasn't spiritual, but wore a cloak

of red and blue taffeta trimmed with mink.
I never once saw him buy a man a drink

despite the wealth he'd totalled from the plague.
'Gold's good for the heart!' was all he cared to say.

Hospitals

after 'Hospitales', Victor Rodriguez Nunez

Whose hand is this that steers
the patients of Yarini Pavilion
as they proceed to breakfast
each and every morning of their deaths?

Their pyjamas are too short,
almost without exception,
tailored to bodies
resistant to life.

They drink hot streams of milk,
served to them *cantabile*
by this doh–reh–mi–ing black boy
who's so assured, so self-possessed.

The national hero of public health
watches them attentively
from his bust of dark marble,
without commiseration.

Whose hand is this that steers
the patients of Yarini Pavillion
as they proceed to breakfast
each and every morning of their deaths?

Behind them dust motes swirl
in shafts of sunlight, advancing
on parade. Disinterested trees
appear at the grand windows,

closed today before this false
start of the island's winter.
The dawdling matron,
refulgent, tags along behind,

a great nostalgia between her legs.
All ascension is inevitable.

A Blind Man

after 'Un Ciego', J.L. Borges

I do not know whose face appears
whenever I gaze in the mirror;
nor do I know the ageing man who nears
himself in tired and silent anger.

Slow in my blindness, my hand explores
his hidden features, until a light takes hold
of me and gives a glimpse of his hair
the colour of ash, now tinged with gold.

I say again that I have lost no more than
the empty surface of things—
this spirited wisdom is Milton's—
but then I think of roses and of writing.

I think if you could see my expression
you'd tell me who I was this perfect noon.

I, Me, Myself

after 'Yo', J.L. Borges

The skull, the secret heart,
the brooks of blood I never see;
tunnels of sleep, that shape-shifter;
bowels, bones, the nape of the neck:
I am all these hidden things. Incredibly
I am also a memory of the sea
and a solitary west-bound sun
spent in gold; in shadow; nothing.
I am he who watches boats from port.
I am countless books and numbered
engravings washed out with time.
I am he who envies the foregone dead.
How weird it is to be the one who weaves
words in some room of a fleeting house.

The Wounded Child

after 'La muerte Del Niño Herido', Machado

Again in the night, the hammering
fever behind the kindly bandaged eyes
of the child: 'Mama, the yellow bird sings!
Look, the black and purple butterflies!'

'Sleep now, son.' Beside the bed she
presses his slight hand: 'Oh fiery flower!
Who can cool you, flower of my blood, tell me?'

Lavender perfumes the drab chamber
while outside the fat moon sheds
light on the domes and the city's bleak towers.
An invisible aeroplane drones overhead.

'Are you asleep, sweet bloom of my blood?'
The glass in the balcony windows shudders...
'Oh cold, cold, cold. So cold!'

Cremation

after 'Incineración', Juan Antonio Villacañas (1922–2001)

As always, the evening;
as always, the night,
or the morning. As always,
we wake, reminding ourselves
'It's day all day today.'

We call a day twenty four hours; something
we've invented to convince ourselves
that, somehow, we still exist
while those of us who've died
no longer do, strangled
by the same old time,
      as always,
           so punctual.

'They will be the ashes death makes sense of,'
      the poet says.
           I find that hard to believe.
Poets don't know what they're talking about.

Morning, evening, night and death. Anywhere.
That's got more grace to it; more grace than sense.

Poets don't know what they're talking about
when they talk about love,
          when they talk about death…

Your average Joe, all dewy-eyed,
knows more than they know about love.

And any cadaver knows more about death.

So, I say, What do poets know
about this liver failure?

What do they know
about the woman's missing breast,
the nipple-less breast for her child,
the absent breast she can no longer touch
to her own satisfaction?

Cancer knows all about that.

Poor pain… that never hurt a poet in their verses!
Poor thinking ashes!

Love's dust…

where are you?

Tell me then, you messengers of death,
tell me what I should do about this body,
this flesh that gets me round from A to B,
alone,

counting the days,

as always.

A Villanelle in Varanasi

for Sambudha Sen

*In 2017, the population of India was estimated at 1.33 billion
while, every year, India's population increases more than any other.*

*'Scheduled Castes' has replaced the unacceptable designation
'Untouchables'.*

In Varanasi on the burning ghats
the bodies burn through every hour god sends—
from Scheduled Castes to rich aristocrats.

As bodies rattle in on timber slats
the fleeting surface of creation rends
in Varanasi on the burning ghats.

By day lean dogs appear, by nightfall, bats.
The dealer of the pyre-wood likewise vends
to Scheduled Castes and rich aristocrats.

On Gangas' farthest shore the sandy flats
gaze on remotely as the river wends
past Varanasi and the burning ghats.

Three hundred folk a day, you do the maths—
a hundred-thousand-plus by each year's end,
from Scheduled Castes to rich aristocrats.

Here bathers cleanse their souls and cows drop pats—
the ashes, bones, the shit, the soapsuds blend
with Scheduled Castes and rich aristocrats
in Varanasi on the burning ghats.

A Wife Advises Her Husband on His Dreams

after The Nun's Priest's Tale, Canterbury Tales

There's nothing much but foolishness in dreams
and nightmares stem from overeating cheese,
when stomach gas and excess humors mix.
Certainly, these wonders that you've dreamed
were brought on by your surplus of choler,
which causes dreaming folk to be afraid
of arrows, fire and foxes and of strife,
as well as toothy Mastiffs and Whippets;
just as melancholy makes dreamers cry
for fear of black bears, bulls, or of devils
who might abduct them as they lie asleep.
I could tell you how the humors cause
more nightmares, but I won't—as Cato said
'Forget your dreams!'
                              But now the night is here,
please, take some laxative and purge yourself!
I know we don't have chemists in the town,
so I shall guide you to the perfect herbs
growing in our yard which, by their nature,
will flush you out at both ends, top and tail.
Don't disregard this—you're a heated man;
beware the sun at midday, avoid fires,
or I'll bet you a fiver you'll die from
a fever. I'll put you on a simple diet
before you take this buckthorn laxative,
this tincture of ivy that grows in our grounds.
Pick them fresh and eat them as they grow.
Cheer up my love and dread your dreams no more.

Bald's Leechbook

'Anglo-Saxon remedy kills hospital superbug.'
– New Scientist, *30 March 2015*

*The remedy was discovered in an Old English
Medical text, Bald's Leechbook (or Medicinale
Anglicum).*

Pick cropleek and garlic
of both equal measure;
take the gall of a bullock
and pound them together;

mix wine with the mash
and then let it lie
for nine days in brass
to conquer a stye...

or for those who've had a
gall bladder
removed, bile salts
make excellent antidotes.

Self-sterilising, they say.
Better than vancomycin against MRSA.

Acute Myocardial Infarction

after The Knight's Tale, part IV, Canterbury Tales

His chest began to ache. The AMI
traversed his trunk then spread into his arm.
There's nothing we can do, the doctor said,
the arteries are blocked with clotted blood.
Leeches, phlebotomy, nor suction cups,
will serve him any use. No herbal potion
or emetic can expel that poison.

His bronchioles began to fill with fluid,
while every muscle in between his ribs
lay wasted and corrupted. *Vomiting*
won't save him now, nor laxatives purge him.
The man lies shattered; nature has surrendered
her rule. Farewell love! Farewell medicine!
Bear the man to church! It's time to die.

Surgery Operation

a found poem, received as spam email

Greetings, I hope you are fine and sorry for not writing
you before leaving to Liberia to help with my family
that she was diagnosed with blood and X-Rays showing
an 'incidental finding' of tumors in her liver to appear to be

Surgery Operation. The news of her illness arrived to me
as emergency that needs family support to keep her I pray
in the ongoing. But I got the robbery problem on my way,
my credit card, cash and valuables things are vanish suddenly

and now the hospital manager he is demand of a deposit of more
than 20,000 Euros before they carry out the Surgery Operation
to save his life. Please if you can assist me with a soft donation

of 20,000 Dollars for banks to make the needy arrangement before
she died here? I did not take along my phone and it is currently
switched off. I promise to pay you back when I return to my city...

Snake Oil

after The Pardoner's Prologue, *Canterbury Tales*

'Roll up, roll up! Observe this bone, this spell…
if you drop this marrow in your well

the water you draw up from down below
will cure a calf or sheep, an ox or cow

that's swollen up because it ate a bug,
or bore a gadfly's sting. Now, take your jug,

wash the creature's tongue and, hey presto,
it will be cured! You also ought to know,

a ram or ewe that only drinks a drop
will soon be healed of scab and sores and pox.

What more? I hear you ask, *Can it be true*
it doesn't just cure beasts but farmers too?

Fast for a week and then, before sunrise,
drink a draft—your beasts shall multiply,

your riches too. It even cures suspicion!
Imagine if you will a jealous man…

just two drops of this water in his bisque
and he won't accuse his wife of taking risks

with other guys, even though he's sure
she's had it off with two or three or more…'

Five Noses

i. Publius Ovidius Naso (Ovid)

after 'A Una Nariz'
by Fransisco De Quevedo Y Villegas (1580–1645)

There once was a man who was stuck to a nose—
an authoritative nose. Authorish.
It was a superlative nose;
a most hairy swordfish.

It was a poorly aligned sundial,
an elephant inverted;
it was a thoughtful medicinal phial,
a metamorphosed Ovid.

Yes, it was the prow of a proud ship,
a pyramid of Egypt.
It was *the* nose of the twelve tribes of Moses.

It was the summation of all that *is* 'nose'.
Very much 'of a nose', but such a fierce nose,
it would have marred the face of the noseless.

ii. Tycho's Nose

Tycho Brahe, *the 'Dane with the Silver Nose',*
who developed a geocentric model of the solar
system, late C16th.

For want of agreement where maths was concerned
    he challenged his cousin to meet him with swords.

For want of a lamp when their sabres were drawn,
    like a surgeon his cousin removed half his nose.

For want of a muzzle he ordered a jeweller
    to make a replacement of silver and gold.

For want of a nose he became a physician
    dabbling in alchemy, mapping the stars.

But for want of a telescope Tycho could only
    observe the dark heavens with his naked eye

and because of an argument over the planets
    he proffered a model where Earth was the rose

at the heart of the system. Then came Copernicus
    who snipped him from history, like his nose.

iii. Taliacotius's Noses

*after lines from 'The Economy of Love' by John Armstrong
(1709–1779), an eighteenth century guide to sex.*

*Gaspar Taliacotius (1546–1599) was professor of medicine and
anatomy at the university of Bologna.* Curtorum Chirurgia Per
Insitionem *(The Surgery of Defects by Implantations) was
published in 1597. He is celebrated for his nasal grafts.*

What curses they bore! Though now the jinx attacks
with twice the venom, cruelly damaging
today's delinquents; undercutting their noses
and celebrity, in all their tasteless lapses,
warping divine faces with shocking ruin.
They say that nice man, Doctor Taliacotius,
repaired poxy deformities like these,
with proxy noses taken from the deceased,
or hide-thick skin from the calloused rears
of sedentary workers. A risky procedure?
No sooner has cruel luck called for the graft
than just desserts rejects the foreign part:
'Failure due to non-adherent nose.'
Thank god for these new immunosuppressants.

iv. A Leap-Year Nose

after 'Arte Poetica?', Víctor Rodríguez Nuñez

Oh to be done with
my myopic eyes
                this leap-year nose
these lips that can't form kisses
my camel's hair!

I inherited the body of an athlete.
       Retired.

I also got the evil genius
                of my father
the pain in my mother's side
my grandmother's suspicious
mole.
       All of their bad kidneys.

I even got the constant fevers
of my son.

All of which gives me good reason
to hold beauty
            in very poor esteem.

v. Body Poetic

It does not require rhinoplasty,
a tummy tuck, or face lift —
poetry is beautiful
just the way it is.

It doesn't need Botox, steroids,
or to pump iron—poetry
is fit and healthy as it stands.

It doesn't need silicone implants,
liposuction, body contour surgery,
collagen, or hylaform injections.

It has no need for pulsed light treatment,
laser hair removal, carpal tunnelling,
Spider Vein Therapy, or a Parisian Peel…
Non, la poésie est belle juste la façon dont il est.

The Pardoner's Tale

i. To a Doctor

after Words of the Host to the Physician and the Pardoner,
Canterbury Tales

Dear Doctor, may God save your gentle bones,
your spiced wines and your uroscopic flasks,
your dark containers full of honeyed pastes.
God bless them, and our lady Saint Mary!

You seem a decent man and I can't speak
like you but, Christ, your story makes me sad—
I almost died from coronary collapse!

Unless I get a pint of hoppy ale,
or someone sings a cheerful song, I'll die
of pity for the tale you tell. Someone
recount a funny story right away!

'You're on,' the Pardoner said, 'but, tell you what,
let's nip inside this pub—the Pig & Sty—
I fancy a pint and a slice of pie…'

ii. The Ballad of Gallipot Lane

after The Pardoner's Tale, Canterbury Tales

Gallipot: *a small pot of glazed earthenware or metal,*
used by pharmacists to hold medicines or ointments.

As I went out one morning
walking down Gallipot Lane,
I saw a villain buying
a package of strychnine.

He said there were two giant rats
had slaughtered all his chickens
and he would gladly lay a trap
to free him of these vermin.

The chemist then he answered,
'*This* is your lucky day.
I have some stuff that—I won't lie—
will blast those rats away.

In all this world there is no beast
can drink *this* and survive.
You only need the smallest dose
and they'll both surely die.'

The scoundrel then he purchased
a measure of the draft
and hurried off across the town
to buy himself some flasks.

Two flasks he filled with venom,
the third he filled with grog,
before he set to burglary
and filled his sack with swag.

He went to find his fellows
to gloat over these goods
and offered both a bottle...
but they slew him where he stood.

When this was done, then spoke the one:
'Let's drink to our reward
and afterwards we'll hide his corpse
beneath these filthy boards.'

That gangster grabbed a bottle
and drank himself to death.
His fellow too then slaked his thirst
and drew his final breath.

As I came home that evening
walking up Gallipot Lane
I saw three bodies disappear
like runoff down the drain.

The Broad Street Pump

It's summer in the Golden Square.
Crank the lever and watch it pour
five hundred ruined souls or more.

from **Watersong**

Exeter, 1832 cholera epidemic.

i. Ballad of the Coroner

The coroner in frock coat and bow tie
inserts his hands inside the opened skull
to find the brain within is coarse and dry.

Beneath the ribs the pleura are quite healthy,
but both lungs are engorged with blackened blood.
The same is true of both the poor and wealthy.

His scalpel slices through the muscle wall.
The stomach and intestines both distended;
the bladder filled with vitiated gall.

The bowel empty now of gruel dejections;
the urinary bladder greatly shrunk
in each and every one of his inspections.

Before the opened torso is sewn closed
he strokes the black heart—'Flabby. *Ecchymosed.*'

ii. Ballad of the Sexton

It was a sombre morning in the meadow
when the congregation gathered by the graves.
The bulky crowd extended through the gateway
standing in the streets beneath the crosses
set in place to ward away disease.

Respectfully they trailed their reverend father,
who prayed the corpses down the grassy path.
But something stopped them in their mournful tracks…
the digger and his team of burly men
carrying the coffins underhand.

Why won't you carry caskets as you should?
they asked. To which the gravesman said:
I am just a digger and I must make ends meet.
What pestilence may rain on me by carting
caskets high… what of me, my wife and kids?

The angry crowd replied: *Isn't your faith*
worth more than what you earn? and pressing on
their anger spilled into the streets at Southernhay.
What is this bestial burial meted to our dead?
Is Our Lord no longer present to these bodies?

At this the digger stood his ground
and insults streamed like rapids on the Exe:
You Diddikoi, Dipper, you cheating old Duffer,
you rookery Magsman, you Mumper, you Muck Snipe…
you'll get a right Dewskitch, we'll do you right down!

And the angry rabble bore the digger down,
and carried him *hallooing* all the way
to dump him in the Gate House, his voice dying,
the way that a bird's song is drowned
by a sudden downpour of morning rain.

iii. Bury Fields

In Bury Fields the bodies lie
upon the grass in summer time.
The picnickers and students know
this is a place you have to go
to let the days slip idly by.

Where dogs chase sticks and children climb,
the squirrels hoard and blackbirds fly
at liberty before the snows
hide Bury Fields.

And deep beneath, where no one's eye
can penetrate, the bare bones cry:
'We are the Dead—where you now go
we also lived, saw sunsets glow…
sumus cholera perpessae,   *('We are the cholera dead')*
in Bury Fields.'

The Unnameable Taxonomy

'By seeking euphemisms for the WC, we try to deny its existence'.
– *Roy Palmer,* The Water Closet

When man or woman, boy or girl
has to answer nature's call
it may go well if you repeat
this litany upon the seat
with devotion and sincerity:
'The Unnameable Taxonomy'.

    Call it…
    Going to the House of Ease,
    the House of Office, the WC,
    the Thinking Room, the Bog, the Loo,
    the Fortress Of Your Solitude,
    the Boghouse, Jakes, the plain Privie,
    the Washroom, or the Lavatory,
    the Ladies, Gents, the Smallest Room,
    the John, the Can, the Powder Room,
    the Outhouse, Restroom, House of Honour,
    the House of Morning, the Throne, the Crapper,
    the *Garde-robe. Necessarium.*
    The Pot, the Potty, and the Hole,
    the Vladimir. Latrine. The Bowl.

    Call it…
    Seeing A Man About a Horse,
    Disposing Of Your Hazardous Waste,
    Dropping the Kids Off at the Pool,
    An Evening at the Superbowl,
    Having the daily a.m. BM,

Exorcising All Your Demons,
Shooting Out a Game of Craps,
Dropping Anchor, Checking the Pipes,
Catching-up on Some Piled-up Reading,
Evacuating the Crowded Building.

Call it...
Room 101, or Number Two,
Auditing Assets, Doing the Do,
Taking Some Weight Off Your Troubled Mind,
Seeing How Things Turn Out Behind,
Paying The Band, Feeding the Fish,
Call it Making a Special Wish.

Call it...
Bombing the Bowl, Growing a Tail,
Dropping a Biscuit in the Pail,
Planting Corn, Doing the Dog,
Worshipping the Water Gods.
It's Balancing the Daily Budget,
Blowing on the Morning Trumpet,
Putting All Your Thoughts on Paper,
Sparking-up the Ring of Fire...

And when you have intoned this prayer
then you might much better fare.
Unnameable, goodbye to you,
god guide you to a how-d'ye-do
with earth and what the whole world knows:
Now, visit the garden and pluck a rose.

The Flying Toilets of Kibera

*The largest slum in Nairobi, Kenya. 'Flying Toilets'—plastic bags
of excrement—are thrown out of the living area. The names used
here are popular names for Kenyan children, with their meanings.
Globally, some 2,000 children under five die every day from
diarrhoeal diseases due to deficits in water, sanitation and hygiene.*

Because the politicians can't discuss
toilets for fear of breaking taboo,
Afiyah (Swahili: 'well-being, health')
launches hers beyond Kibera's walls.

Because the bureaucrat believes
the settlement must be 'illegal',
Kanja (Sanskrit: 'water born')
slings his to the reservoir's edge.

As plastic bags rain from the sky
Nafula (African: 'born in the rain')
washes his face in the tainted tank.

You choose, Samira... either use the bag,
or squat outside in the perilous night
(Arabic, meaning 'pleasurable place').

on previous books

'A class act. A virtuosic range of formal meters, tone and diction that makes for an impressive collection.'
— *The North*

'Mastering the calmness of a poetical line which bears the past lightly in its arms.'
— *Fortnightly Review*

'A love of language and willingness to play with music, meaning and the reader's expectations and perceptions.'
— *Poetry Review*

'Fine poems, varied in form and subject, assured in their music and beautifully integrating thought and feeling.'
— *Wayfarers*

'A contemporary goliard with an emotional range. The aural landscape that Brown creates is remarkable.'
— *The Bow Wow Shop*

'Smilingly human. A gentle humour pervades, almost Eastern, imbuing the work with humanity and warmth.'
— *Shearsman*

'Brown moves from the lyrical to the analytical with an apparent seamlessness. The work here is full of quietly startling moments.'
— *Poetry Quarterly Review*

'One of our most interesting and exciting younger poets. Work of assured and generous vision.'
— John Burnside